Hughie and the HOLE Through Time

Ali Sparkes   Max Rambaldi

Collins

Contents

The village then and now............... 2

Chapter 1 4

Terrifying toys 14

Chapter 2 16

Houses now and then 28

Chapter 3 30

Tudor clothes 42

Chapter 4 44

Tudor schools..................... 56

Chapter 5 58

Food and drink.................... 70

Chapter 6 72

Messages through time 84

About the author 86

About the illustrator................. 88

Book chat........................ 90

The village then and now

1525

Chapter 1

There was a hole where Spiderman's face should be.

Hughie only noticed it once he'd put on his favourite T-shirt and glanced in the mirror. Instead of Spiderman's cool mask, there was a ragged tear where his chest was showing through.

"Whaaaaaaat?!" he wailed. "How did that happen?" Then he remembered shoving loads of books and games into his wardrobe in a frenzy yesterday. He'd promised to tidy up and then forgotten – until Mum was on her way upstairs to check.

Sighing, he changed into a different T-shirt and went downstairs to put on his trainers.

"Great holey-moley!" said Dad, wandering past and pointing at Hughie's foot. Because there was a big hole in his left trainer – a rip in the silver mesh showing his toe, waggling inside its blue stripy sock.

"What?!" cried Hughie. "That was fine yesterday!"

"You'd better wear the other ones," said Dad.

"But the other ones are nowhere near as cool as these," said Hughie.

"So keep those on," said Dad, shrugging. "Your toe will feel nice and cool."

Hughie grumpily did up his laces and then cheered up as he looked outside. It was the first sunny day in ages. Now was the time to get the pogo stick and bounce along the pavement.

He ran back up to his room and pulled the pogo stick out from under the bed. It was bright blue with red handles and a metal spring down by the footrests. Hughie jumped on, to give it a test, bounced up and down twice in his bedroom – and then pogoed straight into the door.

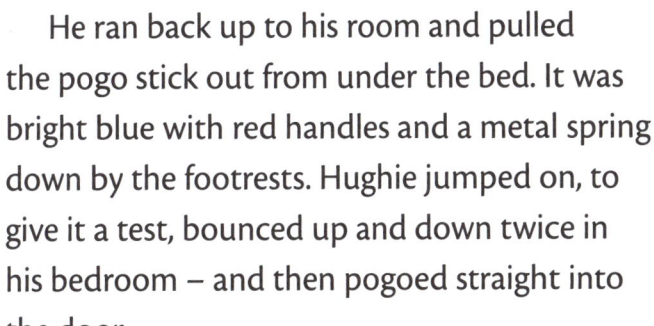

There was a massive thud and a splintering sound. He rebounded, landing on his back, and looked up to see yet another hole. This one went right through his bedroom door.

Mum and Dad came running upstairs.

"Are you all right?" asked Dad, peering through the hole.

"Did you want an extra window?" asked Mum, raising her eyebrows.

Downstairs, Mum put some antiseptic cream on a cut on his elbow and wrapped a bandage around it.

"There's that antibiotic ointment in the first-aid tin," said Dad, carrying bits of splintered bedroom door outside.

"It'll be fine," Mum said. "You only really use that if a wound gets infected." She was a nurse and knew about these things.

"Can I still go and pogo outside?" Hughie asked.

"I think maybe not," said Mum. "In case you fall over again and end up grinding dirt into that wound. Then we *will* need the antibiotic ointment."

"But it's the last day of the school holidays. And it's sunny!" whimpered Hughie.

"You make going to school sound like jumping into the Volcano of Doom," said Mum. "It's not that bad."

"Go and play in the garden ... on your feet," said Dad, coming back in. "And try not to smash a hole in it."

In the garden, the sun was warm on his back and the birds were cheeping in the bushes. Hughie sat down on the swing. Then he heard movement on the other side of the fence – and remembered that new people had moved in a few days ago. Curious, he swung up high so he could spy into their garden.

There was a girl over there.

Swing up! He saw dark hair in tight plaits. *Swing down ...*

Swing up! Wearing a red T-shirt and blue shorts. *Swing down ...*

Swing up! "Hi!" said the girl. "Who are you?"

Swing down ... "Hughie!"

Swing up! "Who are you?" he asked. She seemed to be about his age.

"Kez," she said.

Swing down … "You just moved in?" he called.

"Yep. Just in time to start school tomorrow."

Swing up! "Bad luck!" he said.

"Is Hatchworth School bad, then?"

Hughie thought for a few swings and then said: "It's OK, I suppose. I just … don't like school."

"Yeah," said Kez. "Me too."

Hughie jumped off the swing and sprinted to the end of the garden where a gate led into the woods. "I'm going now," he called back. "See ya!"

He ran along the familiar winding path between the trees. Maybe he should have asked her if she wanted to come, too, but he'd only just met her and –

Hughie stopped. Just the other side of the ancient sweet chestnut tree, which grew next to a large grey rock, was a shimmering sheet of silver.

Who would leave a big round sheet of silver material in the middle of the woods?

Hughie walked on, listening out for people – maybe some kids playing a game. But he couldn't hear anything. Not even birds cheeping.

Well … there was something … a sort of low humming, whispery sound.

Suddenly, every hair on his body stood on end.

Hughie stood stock-still. And then decided he should STOP, TURN AROUND and GO BACK.

Terrifying toys

Everyone's fallen off a bike or a scooter or a pogo stick and got a bruise or graze. But some toys are scarily dangerous!

Clackers

Children in the 1970s were obsessed with clackers – two heavy balls on a thick string. You had to swing them up and down very fast, so they clacked together! But if they caught you in the face, it could really hurt. They got banned.

Lawn darts

Yes – honestly! Big sharp metal darts, that you threw at a target on the grass, were actually sold as a family toy in the 1960s. They caused many injuries. They were banned in 1988.

Kite tubes

These were massive kites that you could fly … with a child riding in them! They were sold in the early 2000s and then banned in 2006 after a series of accidents.

The motorised pogo stick

It's easy to get injured, like Hughie, when using a pogo stick. Now imagine a pogo stick with a petrol motor which can send a fully grown adult waaaay up into the air. They were so dangerous that they were launched in 1961 and banned by 1962.

Chapter 2

"What's that?"

Hughie spun around to see the girl from next door – Kez – standing just behind him. Now he couldn't run back home. Not while she was watching.

"I don't know," he said.

"Let's check it out, then," said Kez, although she didn't move and he thought that maybe she was feeling scared, too.

He edged closer and saw that it wasn't like any material he'd ever seen. It was swirling as well as shimmering, and it wasn't just silver – it was silver and blue and purple and yellow and green.

"Wow," he heard Kez whisper, behind him. "What is that? Some kind of whirlpool?"

"It doesn't look like water," said Hughie. "Or sound like it – can you hear it?"

"Yeah," said Kez. "It's like whispering and humming ... do you think it's a – ?"

"Portal," breathed Hughie. He'd seen portals in TV programmes and on computer games, but they were just stories ... weren't they? They called them holes in the fabric of –

"It looks a lot like a hole in the fabric of reality," said Kez. "What should we do?"

Hughie looked around. The woods surrounded them as far as he could see, getting darker in the distance. Behind them was the path that led back home in just a few minutes. There was nobody else around.

"We should probably – " he began.

And then Kez ran past him and leapt straight into the portal.

"– wait," Hughie finished, too late, as his next-door-neighbour vanished in a ripple of colour. The whispering went a bit louder and the humming got a bit higher.

He gaped at the portal for a second and then realised there was only one thing to do – go after her. Before he could change his mind or lose his nerve, he ran forward, tripped over a tree root and dived headfirst into the portal.

It did feel a bit like water … or maybe a very cool, silky material rippling all over his skin. The whispering was really loud, while all the colours of the rainbow seemed to dance around him.

He landed with a heavy thud, rolled over twice and lay still. Slowly opening his eyes, he realised he was still in the woods. Behind him, the portal continued to whirl and whisper – although it looked more pink and violet now. A short distance away, Kez was sitting on the ground, looking dazed.

"Are you OK?" Hughie asked.

"I think so," she said. "But I'm really, really hungry. Are you OK?"

Hughie suddenly realised that he was, too. He could eat about three cheese sandwiches and a big bag of crisps, right now, without stopping.

"Let's go back and get some food," he said. "And then we can come and take another look at this."

She nodded. "Yep. Food first. Magic portal second."

They ran back through the woods, glancing over their shoulders several times to see the portal. It was still shimmering pink and purple between the trees.

"Do you think," puffed Hughie, "this might be a dream?"

"Maybe – but I've never been so hungry in a dream!" said Kez.

They reached the gate but it looked different. The wood was chunkier and darker, with bits of rope wound around it. Hughie was puzzled. When had his parents changed the gate? And why hadn't he noticed it earlier? He reached up and took a loop of twine off the top of the gate, which allowed it to swing open.

"You can come in if you like," he said, turning to Kez. "Mum and Dad would like to meet you and say hi, I'm sure."

"OK," she said. "But it's a long walk – "

" – about ten seconds!" said Hughie. He turned back to the open gate and felt his mouth drop open. The house wasn't there. Nor was Kez's house, next door. Or any of the other houses in his street – just trees and grass and a winding muddy track that led downhill.

For a moment, Hughie just stood and looked around him, hardly able to believe what he was seeing. Eventually he noticed a house in the distance – but it definitely wasn't his house. Down a long, green hill, in the middle of some fields, stood a very old-fashioned house made from wood and … what was that stuff he'd learnt about at school? A sort of olden days plaster. Wattle and daub?

"Hughie," said Kez, surprisingly calmly.

"Whaaaaa?" said Hughie.

"See that?" said Kez, pointing to the fields where two small figures were leading a horse. "The horse is dragging an old plough. That's an olden days' thing, isn't it? Nobody ploughs like that these days."

Hughie felt a wave of weirdness rise up and drop all over him.

Kez nodded as if it all made sense. Then she said: "Yep. I think that hole has taken us back in time."

Houses now and then

Modern house

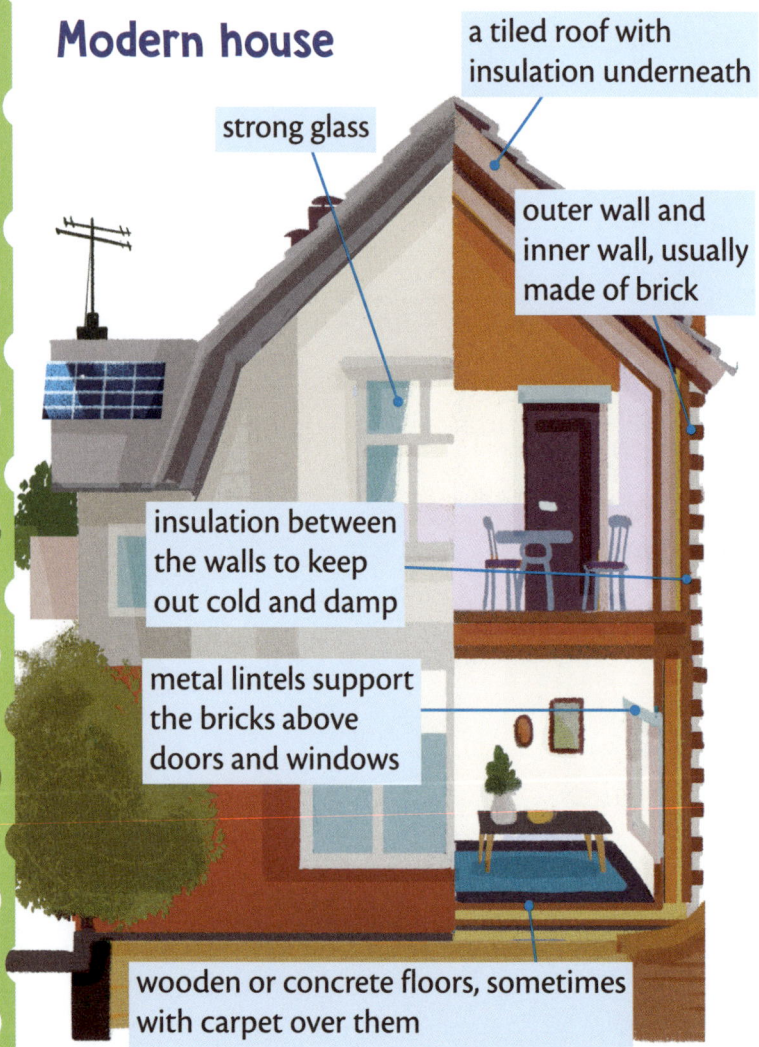

- a tiled roof with insulation underneath
- strong glass
- outer wall and inner wall, usually made of brick
- insulation between the walls to keep out cold and damp
- metal lintels support the bricks above doors and windows
- wooden or concrete floors, sometimes with carpet over them

Tudor house

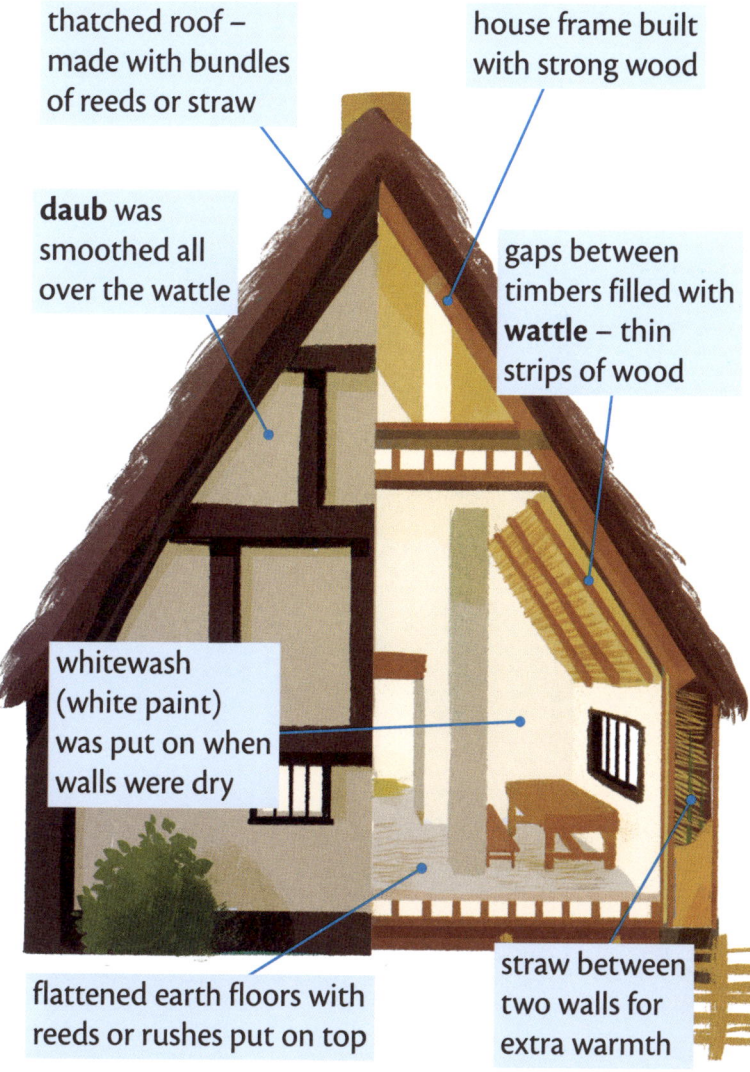

thatched roof – made with bundles of reeds or straw

house frame built with strong wood

daub was smoothed all over the wattle

gaps between timbers filled with **wattle** – thin strips of wood

whitewash (white paint) was put on when walls were dry

flattened earth floors with reeds or rushes put on top

straw between two walls for extra warmth

Chapter 3

Hughie turned around, his heart beating fast. He was thinking they should run straight back to the 21st century – right now!

"We should probably run straight back to the portal," said Kez. "But Hughie … we've got to at least have a little look around first, right?! This is a proper adventure!"

Hughie saw that Kez's eyes were shining with excitement and suddenly he felt excited, too. At least, a bit more excited rather than just scared. "Yeah," he agreed. "We should go and talk to those people with the horse and find out what time we're in."

They broke into a run, along the muddy track and down the hill. The smell was different, thought Hughie. He could smell flowers and grass and a faint smoky tang in the air.

The track joined a road with deep ruts. The road was made of more mud, with straw mixed into it. There were high hedges on either side, with tiny birds flying in and out of gaps in the leaves. Soon, they came to a wide wooden gate which led into the field.

Hughie and Kez stepped up to the gate and peered across it. A shaggy-looking grey horse was walking along the field, dragging an old plough. The plough was carving deep grooves into the brown soil. A boy was steering it.

"Wow! They let a kid do the ploughing!" said Kez.

The boy looked about their age, thought Hughie. And the girl walking behind, throwing oval green seeds into the furrows, was about their age, too.

"Hi!" called Kez, waving at them. She climbed the bars of the gate and sat on top of it, swinging her feet.

33

The two children with the horse and the plough stopped and stared. The girl had red hair under a white cloth hat, and wore an ankle-length brown dress and mud-caked boots. She carried a leather satchel filled with seeds. The boy wore a floppy-brimmed hat of brown material, a grey shirt and brown trousers which stopped at the knees. Below his knees were saggy woollen socks and heavy, mud-caked boots. Both of the young farmers had matching expressions of amazement. Even the horse looked at Hughie and Kez with interest.

"Hi!" said Kez, again, waving. Hughie climbed up next to her and smiled and waved, too.

The boy and girl looked at each other, and then the boy dropped the handles of his plough and walked hesitantly towards them.

The girl followed him, leaving the horse standing obediently in its harness.

"Who are you?" the boy asked, tipping up the brim of his hat.

"And what are they?" asked the girl, pointing at Hughie's trainers.

"Oh, these?" replied Hughie, grinning. If this really was the olden times, he guessed these kids would never have seen trainers before. Especially silver ones with red soles and neon green laces. "They're trainers. Do you like them? There's a hole in that one."

"I've never seen buskins like those!" said the girl, her face full of wonder. "Or such colour on a jerkin! 'Tis passing brave!" she added, staring at Kez's red T-shirt.

The boy looked at Kez disapprovingly and said: "You're showing your legs!"

Kez giggled. "Ah, yes, you didn't do that in the old days. But where we come from nobody worries about that."

"Are you troubadours?" asked the boy. He looked suspicious.

"He means like theatre people," Kez whispered to Hughie. "Or circus folk."

"We're just kids … from another time," said Hughie.

"You're baby goats?" said the girl, suddenly laughing.

"People call children kids in our time," said Hughie. "Um … when is this time?"

"'Tis Wednesday," said the girl, still staring at Kez's T-shirt. "Close to noon."

"No, I mean – what year?" said Hughie.

The boy and girl looked at each other. "'Tis fifteen hundred and twenty-five," the boy said, narrowing his eyes.

"Wow!" gasped Kez. "It's 500 years ago!"

"What is this tomfoolery?" asked the boy.

Kez jumped off the gate and took a step towards him. "Sorry – we don't want to scare you."

"I am not afraid!" said the boy, standing up straight and folding his arms over his chest.

"OK ... so ... who is your king?"

"King Henry Tudor, of course!" said the boy, rolling his eyes just like a modern-day kid.

"Henry the Eighth?" murmured Hughie. "Wow!"

"OK," said Kez. "You probably won't believe us, but we've just come through this ... portal ... through time. It looks like a silvery pool. We come from about 500 years in the future."

This was the point when Hughie expected them to run away, screaming, or maybe get a pitchfork from somewhere and attack.

But they just looked at each other, and then the girl said: "You see, Seth? I told you about the silver pool!"

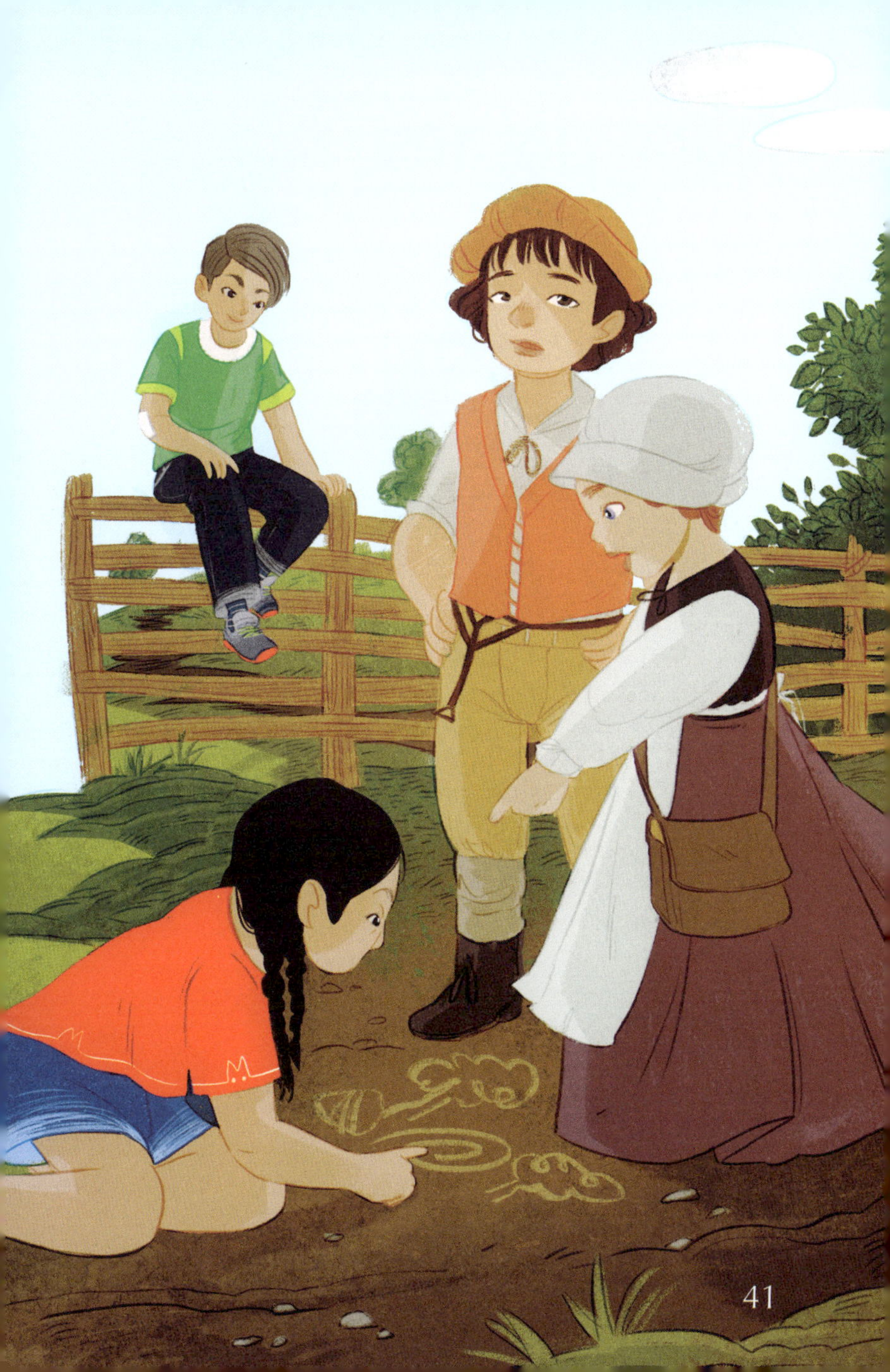

Tudor clothes

Working class people wore clothes like these in Tudor England.

Boy

- cap
- jerkin
- shirt
- breeches
- pouch
- leggings
- buskins

Girl

- biggin
- dress
- leggings
- buskins

People wore cloaks, not coats. Instead of pockets, they had purses or pouches, hanging by string from their belts. Only very rich people could afford bright colours.

Chapter 4

"Wait – you've seen the portal, too?" asked Hughie, jumping down from the gate.

She nodded. "In yonder woods," she said, pointing. "I was scared, so I ran home."

"Show me!" said the boy. "If Linnet speaks the truth, I must see this."

They tied the horse to the gate and went with Hughie and Kez.

"My name's Hughie," said Hughie, as they walked. "And that's Kez. She lives next door to me."

"I am Seth and this is my sister Linnet," said Seth, striding along fast. "And if you try to attack us, I will break your bones."

45

"O … kay," said Hughie.

"What's that called?" Kez pointed to Linnet's white cloth cap.

"Why, 'tis a biggin, of course," said Linnet. "I can't go bareheaded in the sun. Or bare legged." She looked at Kez's knees and giggled.

"A … biggin? Well … OK," said Kez.

"Oak-ay?" puzzled Linnet. "Like an oak tree?"

"Uuummm," said Kez.

"OK means it's all good," said Hughie. "Where we come from."

The brother and sister looked at each other again and Seth said: "If all this is a trick, I will – "

"Look!" shouted Linnet. The shimmering hole was still there, next to the same large grey rock. Hughie noticed a young, slender sweet chestnut tree growing next to it and realised this must the very old one he knew back in the future. It was just a fraction of the height it would later grow to.

"I beg your pardon, sister," said Seth, in an amazed voice. "You spoke the truth."

"We just jumped through," said Kez. "You could, too. Jump into our world!"

Seth shook his head. "'Tis not of this Earth!" he said.

But his sister just jumped right in.

"Whoa!" shouted Hughie. "Wait!" Then he jumped through, too. He landed on the ground in his own time and saw … nobody. "Linnet!" he shouted. Nothing. He jumped back through and found Linnet sitting on the woodland floor. Kez and her brother knelt next to her.

"It cast me out!" she said, crossly, putting her cap back on.

Then Seth leapt into the portal. Three seconds later, he was spat back onto the ground too, looking shocked and confused.

49

"Right ... so it looks like you can't travel into the future," said Kez. "Did you get back through, Hughie?" She looked suddenly alarmed.

"Yeah," said Hughie. "We can do it – but they can't."

"Phew!" said Kez.

"Now you see they speak the truth!" Linnet said, helping Seth to his feet.

"Mayhap," he said, walking around the portal in amazement.

"Can we stay for a bit?" asked Kez. "We'd love to find out about your life! Just for today."

The brother and sister talked quietly for a minute, and then Seth said: "You may stay and help with the planting. If we don't finish, we will go hungry and likely not survive the winter."

"Sure. We'll help," said Hughie, as they set off back to the field. "What are you planting? Potatoes?"

"Po-tay-toes?" said Linnet, wrinkling her brow.

"What are po-tay-toes?" asked Seth.

"This is before potatoes arrived in England?" Kez looked astonished.

"Before chips!" said Hughie. "Before mash or roasties! Wow!"

"We plant beans," said Linnet. "And turnips, later, if we can."

"Don't your mum and dad do it?" asked Hughie. "I mean, I know kids help on farms in the holidays, and before school – "

"School?" Linnet laughed. "What – you think us rich?"

Hughie was silent as they reached the field, where the horse was nibbling at the flowers in the hedge. "So … no school at all?" he asked, eventually. "No reading or writing?"

"Are you high-born in your future world?" said Linnet. She grabbed his hand and turned it over. "Look at these lily-white fingers! Such soft hands have done no work."

"You're no use to us," said Seth, turning away.

"Hey!" said Kez. "We can work!"

"Yeah, thanks for that, Kez," muttered Hughie, five minutes later. Scattering seeds around would have been fine – but Seth had got another, smaller plough with a leather harness that a human could wear. Now Hughie was dragging the extra plough through the earth. His back was really aching.

"Sorry," muttered Kez, as she trudged behind him, steering the plough with one hand and scattering beans from a woollen bag with the other.

"Doesn't anyone you know go to school?" Hughie puffed, as he came alongside Seth and the horse.

"Only the squire's sons up at the manor," said Seth. "Learning isn't for the likes of us. I wish it was. Who wouldn't choose to work with a quill instead of a plough?"

"Oh," said Hughie. "Well, in our time, we all go to school. Even if we don't want to."

"Don't want to?" echoed Seth, stopping dead and giving him a hard stare. "I see now why you dress like a jester. You are indeed a fool!"

Tudor schools

In Tudor England, only the children in wealthy families went to school. Boys went to grammar schools where they learned Latin, Mathematics, Geography and Literature. Girls might learn at home.

Grammar school was hard work. Lessons often started at 7 o'clock in the morning and went on until 5 or 6 o'clock in the evening, every day except Sunday. Teachers would hit pupils with a twig if they made mistakes.

Children in poor families had to work. Boys as young as seven had to learn a trade. And on farms, boys and girls had to do all they could to help. None of them could read or write. They had little hope of getting a better job.

Chapter 5

When the light began to fade, the ploughing and scattering finally stopped.

"Come in and have some bread and drink," said Linnet. They unharnessed Sorrel, the horse, and led her into a barn next to the farmhouse. Brown hens clucked and pecked at the ground as they passed by.

"Will your parents mind us coming in?" asked Hughie, suddenly aware of how odd he and Kez looked compared to these Tudor children.

"'Tis only Father," said Seth. "And he is abed right now."

"He's a bed?" said Kez, looking baffled.

"I think he means his dad's in bed," said Hughie.

"He is ill," said Linnet, as they stepped inside onto a hard earth floor. "Or he would be ploughing with us today instead of you."

"Oh," said Kez. "Is it flu or something?"

Linnet went to a wooden table in the middle of the small, dark kitchen and cut a slice off a round brown loaf. "Father has a fever," she said. "Since he took a cut to his hand."

"A cut?" Kez repeated, taking the slice from Linnet and biting into it. It tasted yeasty and tangy – nothing like the bread at home. "Your dad's got a fever because of a cut?"

Hughie, meanwhile, was staring at the metal tankard that Seth had given him, full of pale gold liquid. He remembered something he'd learned about the Tudors in school. They all drank ale – even children – because it was safer than water back then.

"Um," he said. "Do you have any water?"

"Plenty in the stream," said Seth. "If you don't mind the sickness."

"You know," Hughie said, thinking back to a school Science lesson on fresh water. "Boiled water is safe to drink." He pointed to the heavy iron pot which hung over the ashes in the fireplace. "You make it boil for three minutes and then it's safe."

"Three minutes?" said Seth. "And how much firewood burnt? And who will tend the fire while we're out on the field all day and Father is abed?"

Kez suddenly took Hughie's hand. "Hughie … come and see this!"

Hughie followed her into a small room. A man lay on some straw on the floor, with his eyes closed and a woollen blanket over his thin body. Linnet knelt next to him and undid a bandage. Hughie could see the man's whole hand was swollen and red.

"No wonder he's not helping on the plough," said Kez. "Hughie, we've got to help!"

"You should take care yourself," said Linnet, pointing at the bandage on Hughie's elbow. "In case you take fever." She wiped away a tear. "I've put a herb poultice on it, every day … but still the fever goes on."

Hughie suddenly remembered what Mum and Dad had talked about in the kitchen that morning. "Kez!" he said, leading her back into the kitchen. "We've got to go back and get Mum's first-aid kit!"

"Storm's a-coming," said Seth, looking out through the small glassless window. Dark clouds were rolling across the sky. "Best wait awhile."

"No – we must go. We think we can help your father," said Hughie.

"Whatever you bring through that portal – it's not natural," said Seth.

"Well, is Father's fever natural?" asked Linnet. "Is that what you want?"

"We're going now and we'll be back soon!" said Hughie.

Kez nodded. "Just wait for us!"

Big drops of rain were falling as they ran across the farmyard and up the track towards the woods. Lightning flashed and thunder rumbled.

"My whole body aches!" puffed Hughie, as they reached the woods.

"I know – I'm so tired," said Kez, just behind him. "But Linnet and Seth have to do that every day! And no school or any sort of fun."

"No wonder they're so skinny," said Hughie.

"If they can't grow enough food, they won't get enough to eat," said Kez. "So if they don't get their dad well again to help them … they'll starve!"

The portal looked even brighter in the stormy dark – but it seemed to shudder every few seconds.

"Is it OK?" asked Kez.

67

Hughie suddenly felt scared. What if the portal just vanished, leaving them stuck here in Tudor England? Planting beans and turnips and never eating chips again … never reading a book … never watching TV or playing computer games? And what if his cut got infected and he got a fever?

"Quick!" He grabbed Kez's hand. "Let's go now!"

WHUMP! Hughie landed on twigs and leaves. Kez rolled across the ground to his left.

"Phew!" she said, sitting up. They were both drenched and smeared with mud from 500 years ago. Here it was quiet and sunny. But the portal was still shuddering.

"We don't know how long it'll last," said Hughie. "We'd better do this fast!"

Food and drink

What Tudor peasants ate

Pottage: a thick soup of peas, milk, egg yolks and breadcrumbs, flavoured with herbs.

Bread: dark brown and dense, made from rye or barley.

bread

Rabbit and fish: free meat, if you could catch it.

Eggs: from your own hens.

cheese-making

Milk, butter and cheese: from your cow (or a neighbour's cow).

Pork, beef or chicken: only after you'd killed your own animals.

Dessert

Forget it, sugar was rare and so very expensive. The only sweet stuff most people could get was fruit, in the summer and autumn, and maybe some honey.

To drink

Ale: Even Tudor children drank ale, made from water and fermented barley. It was weak, pale brown and probably didn't taste great, but it was thought to be safer than water.

Pottage was also called pease pudding and there's a nursery rhyme about it:

Pease pudding hot, pease pudding cold,
Pease pudding in a pot,
nine days old.

Yum.

Chapter 6

Mum and Dad were out in the front garden, chatting to Kez's parents over the fence, as Hughie and Kez tore into the kitchen.

Hughie pulled the first-aid box out from the cupboard, opened it and checked for the antibiotic ointment. Yes! It was there, unopened.

They ran straight back to the portal with the box. It looked thinner. And shakier.

"Will we get back again?" asked Kez. They stared at each other for a few seconds. They thought about Linnet and Seth and their poor, shivering dad. Then they jumped through.

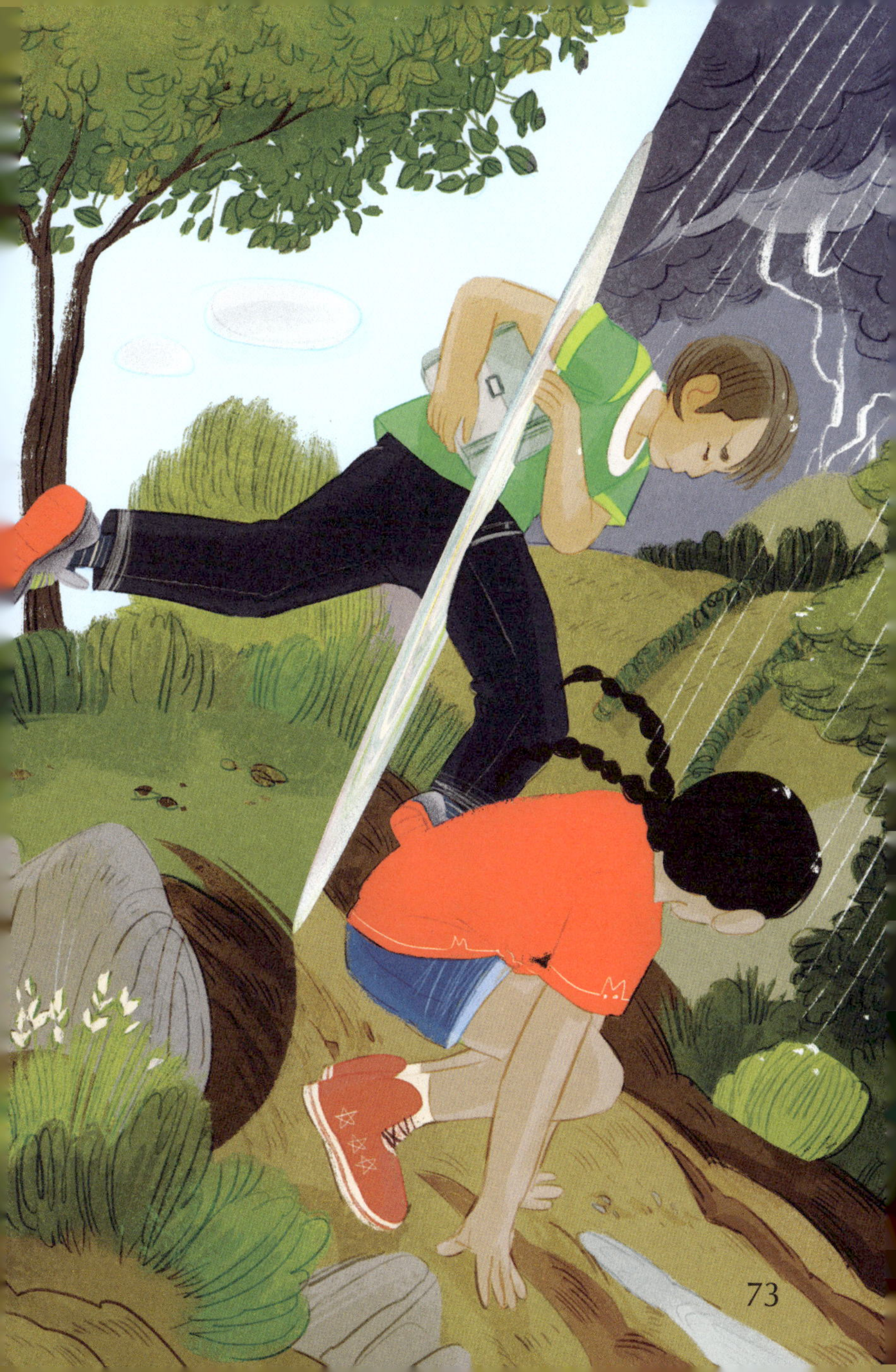

In 1525, the storm was raging. Running down the hill through heavy rain, thunder and lightning, they could just make out the dim light of the farmhouse window. Linnet and Seth must have lit the fire.

They crashed through the door, dripping wet. "We've got special ointment!" said Kez.

Seth prodded at the first-aid box in confusion. "What metal is this?" he asked.

"It's called plastic," said Hughie. "But don't worry about that now. Take us to your father."

Seth took them to where Linnet sat with some hot water in a basin, unravelling her dad's grubby-looking bandage by candlelight.

Hughie remembered what Mum always did. "We need to get it clean first," he said, opening the box. "Here – use this!" He pulled out some fresh, clean cotton wool. Linnet widened her eyes as if she'd never seen such a thing, but she took it, dipped it into the hot water and began to clean the wound.

"You can use this," said Hughie, pulling out a big roll of clean bandage. "But first, here's the special ointment."

Linnet's eyes were even rounder as he took the plastic cap off the tube and squirted some of the ointment onto her dad's cut hand. She gently dabbed it into the wound, while her father groaned and sighed, his eyes still closed.

"Now," said Kez, reading the information on the ointment tube. "You must use this three times a day – every day – until it's all gone!"

Seth stood in the doorway. "'Tis wrong," he said. "We know not where it comes from."

"Seth! We must!" said Linnet, smoothing a fresh bandage on her father's hand.

"It should work," said Hughie. "People hardly ever die from cuts in our world."

77

"Dab it on three times a day," repeated Kez, as Hughie helped Linnet to bandage up the cut. "There's enough bandage to change it every day for a week. And you can wash this material in boiling water, and use it again if you need to, OK?"

"Will it really work?" asked Seth.

"It's your father's best chance," said Hughie. "Now … we have to go."

The run back to the woods was very scary. *What if the portal's gone?* thought Hughie. The hole back into his old life might have closed up, and he and Kez would be stuck here forever.

"Wait!" Linnet ran up behind them, carrying the first-aid box.

"Keep it!" said Kez.

But Linnet shook her head. "We cannot explain this box. When father gets better, he will ask what it is. He will say it's not natural. We can't tell him. We can't tell anyone."

The portal – looking faint and wobbly – lit Linnet's small, pale face. Hughie took the plastic box from her. "I really hope it all works out," he said. "But we probably won't be able to come back to find out."

"If he lives," said Linnet, "I will leave a mark here for you to find." She pointed to the rock beside the sweet chestnut tree. "What mark should I make?"

Hughie thought for a moment, looked at the portal, and then said: "A spiral. Like this hole between our worlds." He drew a swirl in the air.

"A spiral," said Linnet, copying his air swirl. "I will. If he lives. Farewell and be … OK."

Kez gave Linnet a hug before she and Hughie turned and leapt back into the whirling pool of light.

WHUMP!

They lay still on the leaves and twigs, exhausted. The portal had gone.

"Do you think we saved him?" asked Kez. "Saved them all?"

Hughie rolled over and stared at the old chunk of rock. It was covered in lichen and bits of ivy and moss.

They had to go indoors and eat three cheese sandwiches and some crisps before they had the energy to start uncovering the rock to look for a carving. Then they pulled back loads of ivy and scraped off tonnes of lichen and moss, digging down deep, until Kez suddenly shouted: "We did it! We did it!"

And there, at the foot of the rock, carved five centuries ago, was a small, unmistakable, spiral.

"We're doing a Tudors project at school this term," said Hughie, tracing the spiral with his finger.

"Lucky us," said Kez.

Hughie nodded. "Yes. We're really lucky."

Messages through time

The message left in a rock in this story isn't as far from real life as you may think. People all through history have carved messages that have survived hundreds of years. Rock carvings are known as petroglyphs.

In Nevada, in North America, there are petroglyphs made by humans who lived at least 10,000 years ago!

In Western Australia, carvings of people and animals are 30,000 years old. That's ten times older than the pyramids of Egypt.

And in southern Peru, people who lived over 1,000 years ago carved big drawings into the desert floor which can still be seen today. They are called the Nazca lines and can be seen best from up in the air.

About the author

A bit about me...

I live in Southampton, England. I have a husband, two sons, and a large woolly labradoodle who takes me out for walks. I've been writing for most of my life.

What made you want to be a writer?

I was a struggler to start with and not good at reading and writing at all... until I realised that books are a portal into another world. I could open one up and disappear into the pages at any time. I was so excited by that idea that I eventually started writing my own. I wrote a four part series while I was still at school! (But it didn't get published.)

Ali Sparkes

What's it like for you to write?

When it's going really well, I forget where I am and who I am. I'm just happily lost inside my imagination, being each of the characters in turn while I write the story.

Where do you like to write?

I'm very lucky to have a little writing studio at the end of my garden where I can go at any time. When I was growing up I never had my own room, because I have two sisters and we all shared. So when I finally got my writing studio (which I call The Pod) it was amazing! So far I have written 22 books in The Pod.

How did you come up with the idea for this story?

My dog, Willow, was taking me for a walk through the woods and I started wondering whether the woods would have looked the same 500 years ago. Maybe the massive sweet chestnut tree we walked past was only as tall as my knees five centuries ago.

I started thinking about how amazing it would be if I could pop through a time portal and check. That's what I was thinking when I came up with the idea of Hughie and the Hole Through Time.

If you could write another time travel adventure, where would it be set?

If I go on another adventure with Hughie and Kez, the portal may take us all to the Stone Age, or Victorian England or maybe just to the 1950s. Possibly even 100 years into the future! I wonder what that would be like? Where would you like to go..?

What do you hope readers get from the book?

I hope anyone who reads this is interested to find out what their own town or village looked like 100 years ago, or 200 years ago or 500 years ago. If you have a museum near you there might be old maps and paintings or photographs you can look at. I think these are the closest we can get to a hole through time.

About the illustrator

What made you want to be an illustrator?

I've always drawn, for as long as I can remember. When I was growing up, I wasn't sure what job I wanted to do, but I knew drawing was my favourite thing. After I finished school I did an Illustration course at university and that really set me on my path.

Max Rambaldi

What did you like best about illustrating this book?

Illustrating this book was a little bit like going back to school, but learning in a different and more fun way. I particularly like illustrating historical books because I always learn something. At the beginning of an illustration project, I might not know very much about a subject. But by the end I will have learnt a lot through research and drawing.

What was the most difficult thing about illustrating this book?

The best part – learning about the history – is also the most difficult, because I might make mistakes and have to do some more research. But I like challenges, they make you improve, and each mistake is a little step towards something better.

How do you bring a character to life in an illustration?
I read the book and I try to create the character I visualised in my mind. I'm a very visual person, so I have clear images of the story in my mind as I read books. Once you can see a character in your head, it's just a matter of copying them onto paper, like drawing a portrait of a friend from memory.

Do you have a favourite character in this book?
I think Linnett is my favourite, she seems like such a sweet and caring girl. I feel protective over her. I see her a bit like a younger sister.

Did you learn anything about Tudor England while illustrating the book?
Yes, lots! Despite the discomfort of every day life, I really love their beautiful buildings and their way of life. I would like to have a time-travel portal so that I could go on holiday there for a week. It would be great to get back to basics, to try their food and to learn to work on the farm. But then I'd need another holiday in the comfort of my modern house to get over it!

What time period would you travel to if you could choose?
I absolutely adore Leonardo da Vinci. So I would love to travel back in time and visit Italy when Leonardo was alive. I would talk to him and see all his inventions and paintings up close.

Book chat

Which part of the story did you like best, and why?

Did any of the characters change from the start of the book to the end?

What do you think all four of the children learned from their experiences?

If you could ask the author anything, what would you ask?

Do you think this book would make a good film? Why or why not?

How would you sum up this book in one sentence?

Who would you recommend this book to?

If you had to think of a new title for the book, what would you call it?

Would you like to find a time portal? Where would you want to go?

Book challenge:
Make a list of things to put in a time capsule for 500 years in the future.

Collins BIG CAT

Published by Collins
An imprint of HarperCollins*Publishers*

The News Building
1 London Bridge Street
London SE1 9GF
UK

Macken House
39/40 Mayor Street Upper
Dublin 1
D01 C9W8
Ireland

Text © Ali Sparkes 2024
Design and illustrations © HarperCollins*Publishers* Limited 2024

10 9 8 7 6 5 4 3 2 1

ISBN 978-0-00-868109-8

All rights reserved. No part of this publication may be reproduced, stored in a retrieval system, or transmitted in any form by any means, electronic, mechanical, photocopying, recording or otherwise, without the prior written permission of the Publisher or a licence permitting restricted copying in the United Kingdom issued by the Copyright Licensing Agency Ltd, 5th Floor, Shackleton House, 4 Battle Bridge Lane, London SE1 2HX.

British Library Cataloguing-in-Publication Data
A catalogue record for this book is available from the British Library.

Download the teaching notes and word cards to accompany this book at:
http://littlewandle.org.uk/signupfluency/

Get the latest Collins Big Cat news at
collins.co.uk/collinsbigcat

Author: Ali Sparkes
Illustrator: Max Rambaldi (Advocate Art)
Publisher: Laura White
Product manager and
　commissioning editor: Caroline Green
Series editor: Charlotte Raby
Development editor: Catherine Baker
Project manager: Emily Hooton
Copyeditor: Sally Byford
Proofreader: Catherine Dakin
Cover designer: Sarah Finan
Typesetter: 2Hoots Publishing Services Ltd
Production controller: Katharine Willard

Printed in the UK.

MIX
Paper | Supporting responsible forestry
FSC™ C007454

This book is produced from independently certified FSC™ paper to ensure responsible forest management.

For more information visit: www.harpercollins.co.uk/green

Made with responsibly sourced paper and vegetable ink

Scan to see how we are reducing our environmental impact.

Acknowledgements
The publishers gratefully acknowledge the permission granted to reproduce the copyright material in this book. Every effort has been made to trace copyright holders and to obtain their permission for the use of copyright material. The publishers will gladly receive any information enabling them to rectify any error or omission at the first opportunity.

p70t Geogphotos/Alamy, p70c Brian Gibbs/Alamy, p70b Gary Perkin/Shutterstock, p71t Chalermpon Poungpeth/Shutterstock, p71b David Pimborough/Shutterstock, p84 Atmosphere1/Shutterstock, p85t Bill Bachman/Alamy, p85b Fotografias de un viajero/Shutterstock.